MW01229815

How to Find Hope and Strength as You Overcome Narcissistic Abuse

How to Find Hope and Strength as You Overcome Narcissistic Abuse

GUIDED JOURNAL

Kerry Kerr McAvoy, Ph.D.
Lisa Sonni

Stones Roll

How to Find Hope and Strength as You Overcome Narcissistic Abuse.
© 2022 Kerry Kerr McAvoy, Ph.D and Lisa Sonni. All rights reserved. No part of this publication may be reproduced, stored in a retrieval system, or transmitted in any form or by any means—for example, electronic, photocopy, recording—without the prior written permission of the copyright owner.

Printed in the United States of America. For information, address Stones Roll Publishing, 5217 Old Spicewood Springs Rd, Austin, TX 78731

All rights reserved.
Graphics by Arianne Faye Bansig

ISBN 13: 978-1-956631-02-9
First Edition Printed in the United States

Sections

Section 1:

Is this love? Something is wrong in paradise

....

....

....

....

....

....

....

....

....

....

....

Lisa Sonni

You already know something is wrong. That's why you are here. We often look at less abuse as improvement. This is not what real change looks like; this is not improvement. There is no excuse to be abusive. There is nothing about this person or their past that makes their abuse towards you justifiable. Abuse is a choice.

_____

_____

_____

_____

_____

_____

_____

_____

_____

_____

_____

_____

_____

_____

_____

_____

_____

_____

Lee Hammock

Sometimes there are storms in paradise. A lot of people stay in the storm because at least you're on an island paradise and "it's not that bad all the time". But if your house keeps getting destroyed by the storm are you going to continue to rebuild it over and over?

Kelsey Straatmann

When something feels ALMOST perfect, but not quite right, this is usually your gut trying to warn you. If something feels "off" it usually is.

_____

_____

_____

_____

_____

_____

_____

_____

_____

_____

_____

_____

_____

_____

_____

_____

_____

_____

_____

_____

_____

Rossana Faye

Love is a verb. Love isn't what they say to you it's how they show up for you. If you feel like actions do not match words, then that "paradise" you felt in the beginning wasn't genuine.

_____

_____

_____

_____

_____

_____

_____

_____

_____

_____

_____

_____

_____

_____

_____

_____

_____

_____

_____

Julia Wong

Actions are sometimes said to speak louder than words. This is absolutely true. However, I believe that patterns are louder than actions because that's when they consistently show you who they really are.

Dr. Kerry McAvoy

The truth can be one of the hardest and bravest things to face, but ignoring it is so much worse because then here's no chance of change.

Section 2:

Help, I'm drowning in pain! Trapped and unsure what to do next

....

....

....

....

....

....

....

....

....

....

....

Lisa Sonni

Feeling trapped is often a fear of the unknown. The unknown doesn't have to be scary. Can you view it as exciting? The pain you feel right now is familiar to you because you have felt it for so long, but this pain is temporary. Decide that you don't want to live in pain, that you don't want to feel trapped. Decide to be free. Indecision is a decision.

Lee Hammock

If you're drowning in pain then it's time to swim to the shore or get close enough to the shore where you can touch the bottom. Write down the TRUTH of your situation and be real with yourself. This may hurt to write down and read what you've been through but it helps make it clear.

_____

_____

_____

_____

_____

_____

_____

_____

_____

_____

_____

_____

_____

_____

_____

_____

_____

_____

_____

Kelsey Straatmann

Learn HOW and WHERE the words "yes" & "no" feel in your body. Ex: when you're happy and excited, where do you feel this? When you're uncomfortable and don't want to do something, where do you feel this? This way when a situation arises and you're feeling trapped and indecisive, your body will tell you how to proceed.

Rossana Faye

HOPE stands for Hold On Pain Ends. Have hope that this painful space you're in is going to end. When you gain clarity, it will hurt a lot, and hurt some more and then one day it won't. I promise you this is temporary, just hang on.

Julia Wong

How long have you been suffocating? Can you really see yourself doing this forever? Rather than staying in a toxic relationship and feeling alone, it's better to be alone and heal. Remember that you were once happy without them, so you can certainly be happy without them again. If you survived the abuse, you'll survive the recovery.

Dr. Kerry McAvoy

Ask yourself what are you afraid of? Then listen with both ears and an open heart. Most likely you will hear the path you need to take.

Section 3:

Ok, enough of this! Creating an exit plan

....

....

....

....

....

....

....

....

....

....

....

Lisa Sonni

Start with small steps if the big ones feel overwhelming. Leaving is never as easy as walking out the door. Create a plan, wether it is short or long term. Remember that the life that awaits you has the potential to be the greatest to be the best life you've ever lived. You just have to take the actions needed to build that future.

Lee Hammock

Leave in the safest way possible. Don't share your plan with anyone that may tell the person you're trying to escape from.

Kelsey Straatmann ──

Once you make a decision stick with it; do not let yourself be persuaded. Write down the reasons why you're leaving and read them whenever you're feeling conflicted or hoovered.

_____
_____
_____
_____
_____
_____
_____
_____
_____
_____
_____
_____
_____
_____
_____
_____
_____
_____
_____
_____

Rossana Faye

The best way to accomplish any goal in life is with 100% intention. When you have 100% intention the mechanics do not matter. You are naturally in action. Planning, preparing, saving, adjusting, all of this happens from a place of determination. You can do this.

Julia Wong

Always remember that your safety is first.

Dr. Kerry McAvoy

There is no wrong way to leave, just your way.

Section 4:

How do I restart again? Reclaiming & rebuilding a new life

....

....

....

....

....

....

....

....

....

....

....

Lisa Sonni

Let go of the self-limiting beliefs that you cannot do this. You absolutely can. Shift your mindset and be conscious of how you speak to yourself. Shift from "I can't do this" to "I am learning how to do this". Write down your goals and dreams; what is the life you've always wanted? Break this down into steps and then take action on each item.

_____

_____

_____

_____

_____

_____

_____

_____

_____

_____

_____

_____

_____

_____

_____

_____

_____

_____

Lee Hammock

This can be an extremely stressful time but YOU get to do what YOU want to do now! How long were you under the control of someone else? You get the life that YOU want now. It's not the end of the world, but the beginning of one.

Kelsey Straatmann

One day at a time. Sometimes one hour at a time. You are strong. You are brave. You are WORTH IT.

Rossana Faye

Welcome to your FREEDOM. Choose a freedom date that signifies the day you put yourself first. Enjoy every moment, celebrate every act of self-love, you get to be fully self-expressed and free now. Remember that your worst day on the side of freedom will still be far better than the best day you ever had with them.

Julia Wong

Look how far you've come! I am so proud of you! Now you have your life back, you have your freedom, you have your power back! Go and enjoy some YOU! Everyone's healing journey is different, so be patient with yourself. Taking it day by day is the key. You got this, and we got you.

Dr. Kerry McAvoy

Beginning again sounds bigger than it is. It's happening every second of every day. Who you are right now isn't who you were yesterday.

_____

_____

_____

_____

_____

_____

_____

_____

_____

_____

_____

_____

_____

_____

_____

_____

_____

_____

_____

Section 5:

Who am I now?
Rediscovering the new you

....
....
....
....
....
....
....
....
....
....
....

Lisa Sonni

Who do you want to be? What are the actions and behaviours that demonstrate this kind of person? The inner voice that often holds you back is not yours; you have learned to feel this way. You can unlearn this; you can block that negative voice.

_____

_____

_____

_____

_____

_____

_____

_____

_____

_____

_____

_____

_____

_____

_____

_____

_____

_____

_____

_____

_____

_____

Lee Hammock

You're a thriver now. You made it out and THAT'S huge. You can get back to an even better version of who you were before/during the relationship dynamic. Take your time, don't rush the healing process and take time to discover and build a new you.

Kelsey Straatmann

GET TO KNOW YOURSELF AGAIN: (*write it down*)what are your foundational morals, values, beliefs? (Religious , political, cultural beliefs, etc) What do you like to do for fun? If you don't know, what are things you USED to do for fun?What are things you don't like? Are there things you've been conditioned to "like" you really don't ?What's something new you've always wanted to try or buy or place you've wanted to go but we're never "allowed" to? What do you LIKE about yourself? What are you GOOD at?

Rossana Faye

That little flickering glimmer of light that they dimmed and tried to put out is still there. It's always been there, just waiting to shine again. You're ready to shine so bright. You are out of the darkness now and ready to step out into the world again as your authentic self. Notice what makes you smile and what excites you. Pay attention to the things that grab your interest. Remind yourself that YOU ARE BACK.

Julia Wong

Grab a calendar and write down one thing you want to do for yourself every day that you couldn't do when you were stuck, and do that one thing for yourself every day! Be sure to take yourself out on a date and get to know YOU again!

Dr. Kerry McAvoy —

Begin with the small things, like a favorite color, song, or food. View yourself like an undiscovered country that you're exploring and have fun with it.

Please follow us on Instagram

Lee Hammock (mentalhealness)
Lisa Sonni (_stronger_than_before_coach)
Kelsey Straatmann (kp_straatmann)
Julia Wong (heartswithjules)
Rossana Faye (_rollercoasteroflove)
Dr. Kerry McAvoy (kerrymcavoyphd)

Made in the USA
Columbia, SC
18 October 2022

69649270R00043